W d the
M Go?

Contents

Chapter 1

The Siesta

The day was hot, but Tomasina Sanchez paid no attention as she skipped along the road, stopping now and then to pick wild flowers for her grandmother.

Tomasina was travelling with her parents, her brother Pablo, and their old red dog Rufo, to the village where Mother had grown up. Tomasina was excited, because tomorrow was the fiesta, and there would be music, dancing, storytelling, and plenty of good food.

Suddenly, the soft sounds of the jungle were split with the roar of a howler monkey from the dense canopy above.

Rufo barked and darted off into the trees, in search of the monkeys.

"Rufo!" Tomasina called. She left the road to chase the shaggy dog.

"Tomasina, stop!" Mother called. "He'll be all right."

"I'll get her," Pablo said. The children disappeared into the rainforest, leaving Mother and Father alone on the side of the road.

It felt cool in the jungle as Tomasina pushed through the large-leafed plants.

She was very careful to keep her new dress clean. It was made of a beautiful white cotton cloth that Mother had woven on her loom and decorated with bands of colourful designs.

Pablo joined her as she finally reached Rufo. He was barking at a troop of howler monkeys bouncing in the branches high above.

The children grabbed Rufo just as Mother and Father arrived. "Perhaps this would be a good time for our siesta," said Mother, who was relieved to find the children safe.

"I know a good place," Father said. "It's just a little further."

He led the family through the forest. Tomasina saw two huge mounds of rock rise up from the forest floor. The mounds were covered with vines and plants, but here and there carved rocks showed through. And there were more carved rocks scattered around on the ground.

"Are these mountains?" she asked.

"No, this is the ruin of an ancient Mayan city," Father answered.

"Everything looks broken," Tomasina said. "What happened here?"

"The Maya left this city, and many others like it, a long time ago," Father said. "It's a mystery, because no one really knows why they left."

Mother spread out her cloth on one of the large, flat rocks. Tomasina ate her lunch of beans wrapped in corn tortillas,[1] and then settled down for an afternoon nap. "How strange," she yawned. "I wonder what happened to them…"

She drifted off to sleep.

1. tortillas – round, thin, flat cakes made from cornmeal or wheat flour

Chapter 2

The Royal Palace

Standing in his doorway, Ah Cacau watched the first light appear in the eastern sky. His room was high above the other buildings, and he could look across the city to the jungle.

His city was in the heart of the Central American rainforest, and his people were the Maya, a proud race of dark-skinned men and women.

Ah Cacau was up early because it was the festival day for Yum Kax, the god of corn. That afternoon, the ceremonial First Seed Planting would take place. But, first, there would be music and dancing, storytelling and ball games.

Ah Cacau planned to see it all, but not with servants watching him closely. No, today, he would be a normal boy, doing normal things.

For Ah Cacau was not an ordinary boy – he was the most important boy in the city. He was the Ahau, the young prince. His father, Ah Jaguar Shield, was king. Someday Ah Cacau would be king, and he was sure he'd be a better ruler if he knew what ordinary boys were like.

Ah Cacau looked around. Most of the household were still sleeping. But down in the cooking rooms, teams of servants were preparing the royal family's meals.

The prince got out his oldest and plainest clothes and sandals. He wrapped a woven cloth around his waist and threw a shawl over his shoulders. He thought about his long, black hair. Usually, his servant arranged it in an elaborate style, but today he would let it hang loose, as most of the Mayan men did.

He climbed down the steep staircases, from one terrace to another. Finally, he reached the street and breathed a sigh of relief. Now he was safe. No one would recognize him.

Ah Cacau walked past buildings where city nobles worked. He passed the homes of nobles, scribes,[2] astronomers, and other important men. Towering above the city were the twin temples, where the priests lived and performed rituals.

The streets finally opened on to a large, open square – the plaza. He had been here before but, today, this early in the morning, it looked different. As well as the festival, this was a big market day.

Many of the traders had come from faraway places and had slept on the streets the previous night. And now, as the sun rose, they set up their booths, lashing poles together and draping them with cloth.

"Hey, boy!" one trader yelled. "Make yourself useful or get out of the way."

Ah Cacau thought this loud, rude man was surely from another land.

2. scribes – people from the upper, educated class who wrote, copied books, and taught the children of nobles

He didn't have the flat broad head, high sloping forehead, and long beaky nose that all the Maya had.

Ah Cacau moved on. He watched the people stream into the city. They came once a week to sell, or trade, their corn and squash, peppers and beans, potatoes and woven cloth. Everything was displayed in colourful pots or baskets.

As the sky grew lighter, the activity in the market increased. Turkeys gobbled and parrots squawked. Men, women, and children jammed the plaza. They examined wares, haggled with traders, and chatted with friends. Ah Cacau had to remind himself not to stare. He had to look as though he belonged.

Chapter 3

The Search

Back at the palace, the rest of the royal family was now awake. The servants ran this way and that.

"Where is the Ahau?" one shouted.

"How should I know? You slept outside his room."

"We'll have to tell Lady Kanal Ikal."

Lady Kanal Ikal was Ah Cacau's mother. She was dressing for the festival as the servants rushed in. She clasped a heavy necklace of jade beads around her neck as she said, "What do you mean my son is missing? Find him!"

"We've looked everywhere, Lady. He is nowhere to be found."

Despite the weight of her jade earrings and necklace, belt of rare stones, and hair filled with heavy ornaments, Lady Kanal Ikal ran to the passageway.

"We must inform Ah Jaguar Shield at once," she said to the terrified servants.

The servants trembled as they followed the queen through the palace.

When they reached Ah Jaguar Shield's chamber, Lady Kanal Ikal said, "Our son is missing."

"What?" roared the king. "I'll have these foolish servants' heads for this!"

"Calm yourself, my husband. The servants have searched the palace and are as concerned as we are."

"Our enemies must have stolen Ah Cacau. They want to go to war," Ah Jaguar Shield said. He was also dressed; he had yellow and purple cloth twisted around his head, and the royal green quetzal bird plumes in his turban bounced up and down as he walked.

"We must call the high priest," the king said forcefully.

The high priest came in, wearing an alligator head as an elaborate headpiece. "I looked into the sacred smoke," he assured the king and queen. "I saw a vision of Ah Cacau in a crowd of people."

"Perhaps he escaped his captors," Lady Kanal Ikal said hopefully.

"Or perhaps he was never captured," the priest said.

Ah Jaguar Shield was angry. "Are you saying my son ran away? He would never do that. He knows he will be king one day." Ah Jaguar Shield called for the royal guards. "Find my son," he ordered them. "Capture anyone who is holding him."

The four soldiers, with their brightly painted faces and fierce looking headpieces, bowed their heads and marched out.

Chapter 4

In the Plaza

Tokla sat on the ground with her loom in her lap, finishing the cloth she hoped to sell in the market. It was the first piece she had done without Mamá's help, and she was proud of her work. She had spun, dyed, and woven the cotton into an elaborate design.

As she worked on her cloth, Tokla watched while her mamá prepared the family breakfast of flat corn tortillas. She cooked them over the hot stones on the hearth.

Tokla's brother Pacal had gone with Papá to their fields down by the river to gather bananas and avocados to sell.

The baby cried, and Tokla lifted her from the hammock. She was a pretty baby, Tokla thought. She was brown, like all Maya, and had straight black hair and a nice flat head. When she was very young, Mamá had strapped a wooden board to the back of her head to make the forehead slope back. When the men entered the house, Mamá fed the baby while Tokla served the breakfast.

When the family left home, the sun was just turning the sky pink. It would be hot today, Tokla knew. No rains would cool the heat. This was still the dry season – the time for the First Seed Planting ceremony later in the day.

Tokla and all her family were dressed in their best clothes to honour Yum Kax. She and her mamá wore loose white dresses, but no jewellery like the noble women. Mamá carried the baby slung on her back. Tokla had woven yellow fabric around her four short braids.

Papá and Pacal wore cloths around their waists. No one in the family wore shoes. Shoes were for nobles. Papá, Pacal, and Tokla carried bananas and avocados on their backs, wrapped in cloth strapped to their foreheads.

"Good morning," they called to their neighbours, who were all heading to the market. "Happy festival to you."

"That's a fine crop of avocados!" someone called back.

Tokla looked around as the family entered the city. Its beauty always amazed her. The buildings were constructed of stone. Many were painted with pictures of birds or snakes, all in greens, reds, yellows, and blues. In the plaza, the twin temples rose as high as mountains.

"We'll set out the fruit here," Mamá said. Then she said to Tokla and Pacal, "As soon as you sell what you brought, you can go and have fun."

Tokla was excited. One of the traders bought her cloth straight away.

Pacal sold the last of his avocados as a boy of about twelve stopped, and asked for a banana. Pacal looked at him curiously. The boy was dressed as a peasant, but was wearing the sandals of a noble. As the boy turned to leave, Pacal called out, "Hey, wait. My sister and I are about to go off and explore. Do you want to come with us?"

The boy grinned and said, "Yes. I'm Cacau. Who are you?"

While Tokla and Pacal introduced themselves, Mamá handed them a gourd. Inside were warm tortillas filled with turkey and deer meat. "For your lunch," she said. "There should be enough for three of you. We'll look for you at the ball court before the games."

Chapter 5

The Market

The four soldiers from the palace marched through the city, their feet clacking on the stone pavement. "Has anyone seen Ah Cacau, the young lord?" they called.

"He was taken while he was sleeping. There's a reward for anyone who finds him, or the enemies who took him."

This gave the crowd something new to talk about. What had happened to the Ahau? Were they about to go to war?

The soldiers marched on, turning into each street and alley.

Ah Cacau pulled his friends around the corner, away from the soldiers.

"Who are you really?" asked Pacal. "Are those soldiers looking for you?"

Ah Cacau was silent.

"You can trust us," Tokla said.

Pacal reached under the shawl Ah Cacau was wearing and pulled out a necklace with a gold bell. "You must be a noble," he said. "No peasant has anything like this."

"And you have carved teeth," Tokla added, nodding at Ah Cacau's teeth, which were filed into zigzag points.

"You're right," Ah Cacau said. "I am hiding from the soldiers. I am Ah Cacau, the son of Ah Jaguar Shield."

"The king's son!" Tokla and Pacal couldn't believe their ears.

"Yes. I wanted to spend one day as common boys do, to learn what they do and think. I can't do that with servants surrounding me. I think it will make me a better ruler if I can understand what people are like."

"I'm honoured that you chose us," Pacal said. "But if you really want to hide, you'll need to cover your mouth, and take off that shawl and those sandals."

"That gold necklace has to go, too," Tokla said. She looked at the corner of the building and pulled out a loose stone. "Let's hide it in here. We can come back for it later."

The three of them joined arms and walked through the market plaza without fear. If Ah Cacau kept his mouth closed, no one would know who he was.

They looked in wonder at everything the traders had to offer: jaguar skins, cacao beans, pottery, carvings. From distant coasts, they saw salt and shells which merchants had brought up the river in large ocean canoes.

"Look at the caged animals," Tokla said. The children went over to a booth set in the shade of the buildings. Iguanas were heaped into one wooden cage.

“Why are these animals here?” Tokla asked the merchant.

“I am selling them,” the merchant replied. “Would you like a tender young iguana to take for your family’s dinner?”

"Dinner!" Ah Cacau exclaimed. "But those iguanas are alive."

"They won't stay fresh for very long if they are dead," the merchant said.

"What about those macaws?" Pacal asked, pointing to some large, colourful birds. "Are those for dinner, too?"

"You couldn't eat a macaw," Ah Cacau cried. "I have one for a pet."

Tokla and Pacal pulled Ah Cacau from the booth. "Sh..." whispered Tokla. "Be careful what you say."

As they walked, Pacal said, "You know, I work in the fields, and Tokla works in the house. But we don't know what you do, Ah Cacau."

Ah Cacau said, "I spend much of the day studying. I study the stars and the planets. I learn about all of the gods. I also learn reading, writing, and mathematics."

"I know some mathematics," Pacal said, "but I can't read."

"Read something," Tokla begged.

Ah Cacau led them to a monument near one of the temples. There were many stelae[3] here, like small stone trees planted in a grove.

"These," he said, "tell our history. They tell about kings, and wars, and all the important events." Ah Cacau pointed to a carving. "This is an image of my father. All my ancestors are recorded."

Pacal said, "And some day there will be a stela with your image, too."

Just then, the soldiers walked past.

"Let's go," Tokla whispered. "They are a little too close for comfort."

"I agree," Pacal said. "Let's go to the ball court and have our lunch. We can still get good seats."

3. stelae – carved stone pillars, sometimes up to 5.5 metres tall, on which the Maya recorded their history

Chapter 6

The Ball Game

The prince followed his friends across the plaza to the great ball court. He had, of course, been here before. But he'd sat in the section reserved for nobles.

The three scrambled up the steep stone terraces to the top, where they would have a good view. Soon Mamá and Papá joined them, and the five ate their lunches, which were still warm in the protective gourds.

People flowed into the ball court: nobles, priests, traders, craftsmen, and peasants. It was the most popular event of the day. The players strutted in, proudly showing off their bright costumes.

One team had yellow plumes in their headpieces and the other had red plumes. The players wore leather pads to protect their knees and elbows. They also wore leather around their hips.

The crowd roared in anticipation of a good game. The heavy rubber ball bounced into the centre of the long, narrow court. Each player scrambled to knock the ball to the other side of the court. The game was very difficult because the players weren't allowed to touch the ball with their hands or kick it with their feet. They could only use their elbows, wrists, or hips to strike the ball.

It took a man of great strength to knock the ball down the court. Soon the players were covered with sweat. The red-plumed team was the favourite to win, but was one point behind.

One red-plumed player ran in from the side, slid to the ground on his elbows, and hit the ball with his padded hip.

The ball rolled past two yellow-plumed players, into their side of the court. The red team received two points and the game was over. The crowd went wild, standing and cheering. Even Ah Cacau stood and yelled.

Across the court, in the nobles' section, the richly dressed women stayed seated, chatting to one another. Tokla watched them and saw one pointing in their direction.

"Ah Cacau," she said, "is that lady someone you know?"

"Oh, no!" said Ah Cacau. "That's my mother, Lady Kanal Ikal. Let's leave."

Tokla and Pacal told their mamá and papá they would meet them back at the fields in time for the First Seed Planting. The three friends left the court and ran through the streets of the city.

Chapter 7

At the River

When Tokla, Pacal, and Ah Cacau stopped to catch their breath, Tokla said, "You'll have to go back soon. What will you tell your father?"

"I'll tell him the truth – that I think I'll be a better ruler if I know my people. I'll tell him how good you have been to me."

"Aren't you afraid he'll be angry? Maybe you should go back," Pacal said.

Ah Cacau said, "He can be angry now or later. I want just a little more time. But perhaps I'm being selfish. Do you want me to go?"

"No, no," Tokla cried. "Stay with us as long as you like."

"In fact, since it's so hot, let's hide by the river," Pacal said. "I'll race you!"

"Let's show Ah Cacau our swinging vine," Tokla shouted. She climbed a rock, seized a vine, and swung over the river.

"Look," Ah Cacau laughed. "She looks like a bird flying through the air."

Tokla let go of the vine and dropped straight into the river. Rising out of the water, she shook her hair out of her eyes.

"Come on," she called. "Are you afraid of biting fish?" They laughed.

Pacal climbed up and grasped the vine. From there he waved to his parents, who were just coming across the fields.

Swinging out high over the water he saw something else further down the river-bank that made him tremble. He could see Ah Jaguar Shield and Lady Kanal Ikal carefully walking through the fields. And he saw the soldiers, armed with spears. Pacal jumped into the water and came up, sputtering a warning.

But he was too late. Ah Cacau was already dangling from the vine, visible for all the world to see. He splashed into the water. The vine fell in after him. Pacal waited, but Ah Cacau didn't surface.

In the distance Pacal saw Ah Jaguar Shield start to run. The soldiers ran. Papá ran. Pacal dived under the water and looked around. Ah Cacau was on the bottom, tangled in the vine. Pacal tugged and pulled at the vine, finally releasing Ah Cacau from its grip. He grabbed hold of Ah Cacau's arms and pulled him to the surface. He gasped for air as he dragged his friend to the bank and laid him on the ground.

"Breathe, Ah Cacau, breathe," he shouted as Papá reached them.

Papá took one quick look at the unconscious boy's blue face, then he grasped the boy's head and opened his mouth. He started to breathe into him, over and over again.

The soldiers arrived, with Ah Jaguar Shield close behind. The soldiers reached out to grab Papá and take him prisoner. But Ah Jaguar Shield stopped them.

Ah Cacau coughed and spat out water. Papá helped him sit up.

Lady Kanal Ikal finally arrived and threw her arms around her son. "Thank the gods you are safe! Who are these people who stole you away from us?"

"No one took me," Ah Cacau said. "Father, believe me. These people are my friends. They saved my life."

By this time a large crowd had gathered by the river. So Ah Cacau told the whole story for everyone to hear. He told of his idea to be a common boy for one day, so that he could be a better king.

Ah Jaguar Shield was so relieved that his son was safe, he forgot to be angry. Instead, he said, "My people, let us celebrate. Yum Kax, the god of corn, has really been with us today. My son is alive.

This man," and he put his hand on Papá's shoulder, "is a hero."

"Praise Yum Kax," people shouted.

Ah Jaguar Shield continued, "This is the day of the First Seed Planting. I will plant the first seed in the field of my son's new friends. They are my friends, also."

Lady Kanal Ikal lifted the clay figure of Yum Kax for all to see. Papá handed the planting stick to the king. Ah Jaguar Shield dug a hole with the stick and dropped in three corn seeds, one for the well-being of his city, one for the safety of his son, and one for the prosperity of his new friends.

Ah Jaguar Shield raised his hands and shouted, "Praise to the god of corn. May he bring us many rich crops. We will record this great day on the history monuments in the plaza!"

Chapter 8

The Gold Bell

Tomasina opened her eyes and saw the pile of tumbled rocks. Sunlight crept through the trees. Birds twittered. Insects buzzed. “Where did everyone go?” she asked, rubbing her eyes.

“We’re still here,” Pablo said. “You’ve been sleeping.”

“But there were crowds of people here,” she insisted. “They were having a celebration in this beautiful city.”

“Oh, Tomasina,” Mother laughed. “Perhaps this city was beautiful once, but it’s just a ruin now. You were dreaming.”

“But I saw the young prince drowning. His friends’ papá saved him.”

Father chuckled. "Your imagination will make you a good storyteller one day."

Mother and Father began to pack up their bundles once more. Tomasina was hurt that no one believed her. I'll show them, she thought. She began walking around the mounds.

This was where the ball court was, she thought. That was the palace, and the plaza was over there. She went over to a pile of rocks and began tugging at them.

"What are you looking for?" Pablo asked, as he followed her around.

"The necklace," Tomasina said. "The necklace with the gold bell. I know they hid it here somewhere."

"You're crazy," Pablo said. He watched as his sister pulled out rocks and threw them on the ground.

Suddenly, Tomasina started to wave something in the air. "I've found it!" she cried. "I've found the gold bell – it was here, just like I dreamt!"

Pablo stared at the bell. "How did you know this was here?"

"I saw the children hide it. I told you they were here."

She ran back to Father. "Look what I've found," she called.

Father sat down under a tree. "Come and tell me all about it," he said.

So Tomasina told her family of her dream and how she found the gold bell.

"It was like it just happened yesterday," she insisted.

"Well, it would have happened more than 1,000 years ago, when this was a great city," Father said.

Tomasina still wasn't satisfied. "But what happened to all of those people who lived in this city?"

Mother answered her. "The Maya people still live all over Central America. I am Maya," she added proudly. "That means you and Pablo have Mayan blood in you, too."

She smiled and continued, "I also remember hearing a story when I was a child about a king named Ah Cacau. He was a wise ruler and a brave leader."

"Oh boy," Pablo said. "I'll bet he's the one in Tomasina's dream. Hey, let's get going. I can't wait to talk with the storytellers in your village, Mother."

The family began to walk. On the far side of one of the towers, they found a stela that was still standing. It was covered with images.

"What does it say?" Tomasina asked.

"I can't read it," Father said. "But perhaps, some day, archaeologists will be able to translate it."

"I'll bet it's the story of Ah Cacau, the great Mayan king," Tomasina said. She started looking again for flowers to take to her grandmother.

Appendix – Mayan Facts

About the Maya

- The Maya are Indians who have lived in Central America for thousands of years.
- In ancient times, rulers, nobles, astronomers, priests, and scribes were the upper class.
- Workers, craftsmen, farmers, toolmakers, and weavers were all common people.
- Over 2,000 years ago, the Maya began building beautiful stone cities and pyramids in the rainforests.
- Common people lived outside the city in small wood houses with palm leaves or grass thatch.
- Most religious ceremonies were held in cities.
- People who lived in the countryside travelled to the cities to celebrate religious days, and to sell the goods they had grown and made.

What did they know?

- The Maya were the only Native Americans to have a complete written language.
- They had enormous libraries of books.

- Because the Maya wrote many things in stone, some of their written language survives today.
- Archaeologists have been able to translate about half of the Mayan written language.
- In addition, the Maya were advanced mathematicians and astronomers.
- They had accurate calendars and records of the movements of the planets and stars.

Where did they go?

- The great buildings and cities that the Maya built are now empty ruins.
- Archaeologists are trying to find out why the Maya left their cities almost a thousand years ago.
- When the Spanish came to the area in the 1500s, not much remained of the huge cities.
- Although the ancient cities are deserted, the Maya still live in Mexico and Central America.
- They still plant and grow their crops the way the ancient people did.
- But no one knows what happened to the great Mayan civilization that they left behind.

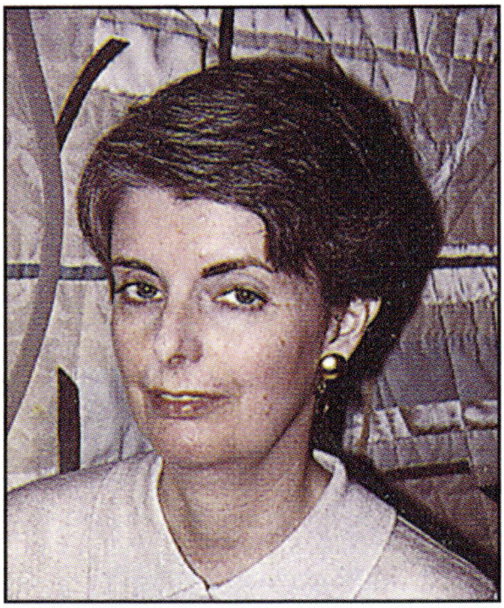

From the Author

I've always enjoyed working with children, first as a teacher, and now as a guide at the Cheyenne Mountain Zoo, where I conduct tours for school children. Because both my father and my husband were in the Air Force, I have lived in Mexico, Morocco, Spain, and Panama. I have also travelled to many other countries with my family.

I now live in Colorado Springs, Colorado, with my husband and a green parrot named Pepito. My two daughters are grown up: one is a doctor, and the other is an artist. I enjoy hiking, music, sewing, and reading.

Cynthia Carroll